DIESELS IN THE
NORTH-WEST

Plate 1: Class 47 No. 47558 is seen working the 17.20 Manchester (Victoria) to Blackpool (North) train, just west of Bolton, on 3rd July 1984.

Paul Shannon

Plate 2: Class 25 No. 25161 arrives at Great Rocks Junction, Tunstead, with the 6H46 limestone empties from Oakleigh, on 4th July 1983.

Paul Shannon

DIESELS
in the
NORTH-WEST

Paul Shannon and John Hillmer

Oxford Publishing Company

Typesetting by:
Aquarius Typesetting Services, New Milton, Hants.

Printed in Great Britain by:
Netherwood Dalton & Co. Ltd., Huddersfield, Yorks.

Published by:
Oxford Publishing Co.
Link House
West Street
POOLE, Dorset

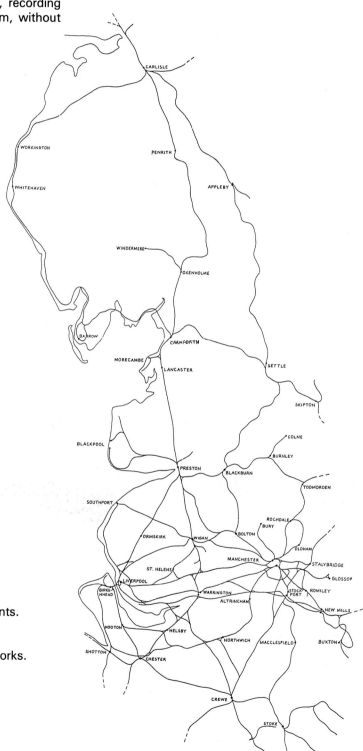

Introduction

From the dense network of local lines in industrial Lancashire to the exhilarating scenery of the Cumbrian Coast and Settle & Carlisle routes, the North West of England is full of varied interest for the railway enthusiast and photographer.

It was in the north-west that steam traction survived the longest - the last scheduled service left Preston on 3rd August 1968 — but it was also in the north-west that some of the first trials were carried out with main line diesels, with locomotives 10000 and 10001 being tested on the West Coast Main Line as early as 1949. Ten years later, the Metropolitan-Vickers Co-Bo units looked set to provide staple power for express freights between London and Glasgow, but their reliability was poor, and they finished their short working life on the Cumbrian Coast line. For many people, however, the Class 50s will be remembered as the principal workhorses of the West Coast route, until its electrification was completed in 1974, and we have therefore included several photographs of these locomotives in service.

Perhaps the most important diesel route today, at least as far as passenger traffic is concerned, is the Trans-Pennine line over Diggle, through Manchester and on to Liverpool. In recent years, all these services have become locomotive-hauled, with many trains starting back from Scarborough and a handful being extended along the North Wales Coast instead of to Liverpool. Another cross-country route, which has only recently been exploited, is that from Sheffield to Preston, via the Ashburys to Miles Platting link in Manchester. The former Harwich to Manchester boat train now runs this way, being extended through to Glasgow and Edinburgh, and there are also Nottingham to Barrow-in-Furness and Nottingham to Glasgow/ Edinburgh workings. Locomotive haulage has brought an improved service to the Hope Valley line, with through trains to Cleethorpes, Hull and York. Further north, a similar upgrading has taken place on the Lancaster to Leeds route, although this is at least, in part, due to the run-down of the Settle & Carlisle railway. The Copy Pit line, too, has found favour once more, with the introduction of regular services between Preston, Blackburn, Bradford and Leeds. All in all, the future looks reasonably bright for these inter-regional routes.

Local passenger services have been worked by diesel multiple units from the earliest days; the first Derby lightweight units having worked between Maryport and Carlisle in 1954. Today, the depots at Kingmoor, Newton Heath, Longsight, Buxton, Allerton and Chester all have their allocation of units, with Class 104 Birmingham RC&W vehicles still working many of Manchester's suburban services.

On the freight side, Warrington has assumed great importance for the marshalling of 'Speedlink' and other wagonload traffic. Its situation is ideal, being both on the West Coast Main Line and approximately half-way between Manchester and Liverpool. Warrington sends trains to destinations as diverse as Carlisle, Healey Mills, Severn Tunnel Junction and the Channel ports, and it is also the main centre for local trip workings in the Chester, Liverpool and Wigan areas. Traffic for the Manchester area is still largely handled at Ashburys Sidings, as it has been since the closure of Dewsnap Yard, near Guide Bridge.

Company and block trains account for the greater part of the region's freight workings, as on the British Rail network as a whole. Vast quantities of coal are carried in merry-go-round trains to Fiddler's Ferry Power-Station, from local collieries such as Bickershaw and Bold, as well as from Point of Ayr, Bersham, Whitehaven and the West Yorkshire Coalfield. Trainloads of coal in HBA hoppers are also received for export at Garston Docks; these originating mostly in the Mansfield area. The limestone quarries at Peak Forest and Tunstead dispatch regular trainloads of stone to various depots around the north-west, including Oakleigh (Northwich), Widnes, Pendleton, Salford (Hope Street), Thorpes Bridge Junction, Collyhurst Street and Stockport (Portwood). An overnight train runs three times a week to Margam Steelworks, and services have recently started operating to Watford Junction and Wilton (Teesside). A great deal of oil and chemical traffic originates in the Ellesmere Port area; Stanlow Oil Refinery, for example, sends trains to Bishopbriggs, Hardendale, Skipton, Leeds, Ecclesfield West, Holywell Junction, Cowley Hill, Rowley Regis, West Bromwich, Aberystwyth and Torksey. ICI chemical trains run from Runcorn (Folly Lane) to Willesden, Burn Naze, Corkickle, Stevenston, Immingham/Grimsby and Wilton/ Seal Sands, from Northwich to Corkickle and Larbert, and from Haverton Hill to Heysham Moss and Glazebrook. Further details of freight services in the northwest are given, wherever possible, in the individual photograph captions.

With resignalling, track rationalisation and replacement of motive power and rolling stock alike, the scene is ever changing. We have felt it worthwhile, therefore, to record a cross-section of the day-to-day working of our chosen area, and we hope you will enjoy this look at *Diesels in the North West*.

Paul Shannon and John Hillmer
1984

Early Diesel Days

Plate 3: A green-liveried Class 45, No. D107, approaches Kirkham with an excursion to Blackpool during May 1965.
J. Davenport

Plate 4: Between 1967 and 1974, most main line passenger turns north of Crewe were worked by Class 50 locomotives, often in pairs. Here No. 435 stands at the north end of Crewe Station.

David Allen

Plate 5: Two-tone Class 24, No. D5053, awaits its next turn of duty at Preston in April 1968.

J. Davenport

Plate 6: On 27th May 1971, green-liveried Class 40 No. 218 arrives at Stalybridge with a Newcastle to Liverpool express.

J. H. Cooper-Smith

Plate 7: Double-headed Class 50s, Nos. D412 and D419, approach Warrington (Bank Quay) with the 14.00 Glasgow (Central) to London (Euston) express on 20th March 1971.

J. H. Cooper-Smith

Plate 8: One of the ill-fated Metropolitan-Vickers Co-Bo locomotives, No. D5702, is seen near Hest Bank with an express from London (Euston) to Workington, during August 1965.

J. Davenport

Plate 9: A busy scene at Carlisle (Citadel) Station, on 13th April 1963. Class 45 'Peak' No. D30 pulls in with a train for Edinburgh via the Waverley route, whilst in the background a Class 40 backs on to a southbound express.

John S. Whiteley

Plate 10: This location has been radically changed by resignalling, track rationalisation and, of course, electrification. On 22nd March 1971, Class 50 locomotives Nos. 438 and 444 head north past Wigan (Springs Branch) with the 'down' 'Royal Scot'.

J. H. Cooper-Smith

Stoke-on-Trent

Plate 11 (above): A cross-country diesel multiple unit, from Lincoln (St. Marks) to Crewe, arrives at Stoke-on-Trent on 28th December 1983. Although the total distance is just under 100 miles, the journey takes over three hours, as most trains call at all intermediate stations, of which there are no less than 25!

John Hillmer

Plate 12 (left): One of the infrequent diesel-hauled passenger trains at Stoke is 1D33, the 08.50 to Holyhead. In this view, Class 47 No. 47456 brings in the empty stock on 27th June 1984.

John Hillmer

Plate 13: The freight lines from Stoke to Oakamoor and Cauldon Low are still in daily use for stone and sand traffic. On 10th April 1984, Class 25 locomotives Nos. 25176 and 25210 are seen at Leek Brook Junction with the 8K02 from Oakamoor. It is now departing for Stoke after running round in the sidings. The HKV wagons are conveying sand for glassworks at St. Helens.
Paul Shannon

Plate 14: The line to Cauldon Low is steeply graded and loaded trains, therefore, are normally worked as two portions as far as Leek Brook Junction. In this view, Class 40 No. 40174 arrives at the junction on 10th April 1984 with the second portion of the 7L82 Cauldon Low to Witton train, conveying gravel in MSV and MTV tippler wagons.
Paul Shannon

Crewe

Plate 15: Although Crewe is at the heart of the WCML electrified system, it is an important diesel centre, with over 150 main line locomotives allocated to the depot. This photograph of the refuelling and stabling point, taken in the early evening of 24th December 1983, shows a variety of types with Class 40 No. 40060 seen on the extreme right.

John Hillmer

Plate 16: A Class 08 shunter, No. 08927, marshals parcels vans on 21st April 1984 at Crewe. At this location, many changes to the layout will occur during 1985, involving closure of the station complex for a period of weeks.

John Hillmer

Plate 17: Most trains to and from the non-electrified North Wales main line change locomotives at Crewe, and on 21st April 1984 Class 47 No. 47456 stands at the south end of the station whilst its driver obtains instructions, after having brought in a Holyhead to Euston service which will continue its journey with electric traction.

John Hillmer

Plate 18: Class 33s have become part of the regular scene at Crewe, working on the Cardiff services. Here No. 33009 backs on to the stock of the 07.12 train from Manchester Piccadilly to the Welsh Capital, replacing the electric locomotive, on 11th August 1984.

John Hillmer

Plate 19: On Christmas Eve 1983, a very wet day, Crewe Station's south pilot, No. 08913, stands in a bay awaiting its next movement.
John Hillmer

Plate 20: Crewe has long been a stronghold of Class 40 locomotives, and on 21st April 1984 No. 40174 draws in from the south with a rake of Mk. 1 empty coaching stock.
John Hillmer

Chester

Plate 21:   Class 40 No. 40092 bypasses Chester Station with 6F27, the 10.13 Penmaenmawr to St. Helens ballast train, on 13th August 1982.

Paul Shannon

Plate 22:   The 13.20 diesel multiple unit service to Manchester (Victoria) stands under the unusual isolated canopies at the east end of Chester Station, on 26th October 1983. The Class 08 station pilot ticks over in the background.

John Hillmer

Plate 23: Renumbered Class 47, No. 47612, is pictured at the head of 1A25, the 06.12 Holyhead to Euston train, on 23rd June 1984, at Chester.

John Hillmer

Plate 24: A four car diesel multiple unit passes Roodee Racecourse, Chester, and crosses the River Dee, as it leaves the city with the 14.44 Manchester (Victoria) to Llandudno service on 8th June 1983.

John Hillmer

Plate 25: Class 25 No. 25135 passes Chester No. 6 box on the morning of 13th August 1982, with a rake of condemned wagons for storage at Mold Junction.

Paul Shannon

Plate 26: At Shotton, on 10th August 1984, Class 47 No. 47329 returns light towards Wrexham after having brought a steel coil train to John Summers' Steelworks, from Llanwern, whilst an unidentified Class 47 locomotive brings an express through the low level station towards Chester from North Wales. There is a regular diesel multiple unit service on the high level line between Wrexham and Bidston, the two levels being connected by a footpath with the booking office situated on the high level line.

John Hillmer

The Wirral

Plate 27: In the heart of Birkenhead's dockland, Class 25 No. 25109 approaches Canning Street North, on 6th July 1983, with a trip working from Cavendish Sidings to Ellesmere Port.

Paul Shannon

Plate 28: On 6th July 1983, Class 03 shunter No. 03189 shunts old-style grain wagons from Chettisham into the J. Rank Ltd. factory in Birkenhead Docks. These vacuum-braked CGV wagons were probably amongst the last of their kind in revenue-earning service, having now been replaced by high capacity 'Polybulk' hoppers.

Paul Shannon

Plate 29 (above): An hour or so later, No. 03189 continues its shunting duties by propelling three 'Polybulks' over the lifting bridge, to reach the northern part of the docks network. These wagons contained grain from Newmarket and Chettisham, and would have arrived on the overnight 'Speedlink' train from Whitemoor.

Paul Shannon

Plate 30 (right): Many oil trains from Ellesmere Port reverse at Hooton before proceeding south to Chester. In this view, Class 25 locomotives Nos. 25257 and 25285 are seen leaving Hooton after performing such a manoeuvre on the afternoon of 6th July 1983.

Paul Shannon

Plate 31 (left): The 16.58 Helsby to Rock Ferry train arrives at Ellesmere Port, on 6th July 1983, worked by a Metropolitan-Cammell unit compriing cars M53208 and M54060.

Paul Shannon

Plate 32 (right): The 13.25 Hooton to Helsby diesel mutiple unit passes the closed Ince 'A' Power-Station, between Ince & Elton and Helsby, on 15th November 1983. One of the few topographical features of the Cheshire Plain can be seen in the distance, in the shape of Helsby Hill.

John Hillmer

Plate 33 (below): Electrification of the Rock Ferry to Hooton line is now under way. Here a four car Derby and Metropolitan-Cammell unit formation is seen arriving at Spital on the 15.31 Rock Ferry to Helsby service on 6th July 1983. Notice how this stretch of line was once quadruple track, the former fast lines being on the right of the picture.

Paul Shannon

Helsby and Frodsham

Plate 34: An unidentified Class 47 approaches Helsby Junction on a sunny October morning in 1983, with 1M58, the 08.50 Scarborough to Bangor 'coast to coast' service. The semaphore signals remain a feature of this busy junction.

John Hillmer

Plate 35: Passing one of Helsby's repeater signals, on 6th July 1983, is Class 40 locomotive No. 40086 with 4H59, the 05.25 Holyhead to Trafford Park Freightliner train.

Paul Shannon

Plate 36: Passing through the sandstone cutting at Frodsham, on 21st June 1983, Class 47 No. 47347 accelerates with a load of empty hoppers.

John Hillmer

Plate 37: Another view of Helsby Junction, showing, in this picture, a double-headed Class 25 freight coming off the Wirral line, on 26th October 1983.

John Hillmer

Plate 38:   A lone passenger waits at the delightfully rural station of Delamere for the 07.24 diesel multiple unit service from Chester to Manchester (Oxford Road), via Northwich, on 28th April 1984. The station is conveniently situated for visitors wishing to enjoy Delamere Forest.

John Hillmer

Plate 39:   On a glorious summer's evening, a few minutes after sunset, Class 45 'Peak' No. 45057 crosses the Weaver Navigation, near Frodsham, with 1J31, the 19.30 Bangor to Manchester (Victoria) train, on 18th June 1984.

John Hillmer

Plate 40 (above): Surely one of the most distinctive freight services in the north-west are the ICI block stone trains which run 363 days a year between Tunstead and Oakleigh, near Northwich. Until recently, most of the 18 wagon trains were worked by single Class 25 locomotives, with banking assistance where necessary. In this view, photographed on Saturday, 10th December 1983, No. 25289 heads 6H42 the 13.15 Tunstead to Oakleigh train, west of Northwich Station.
Paul Shannon

Plate 41 (right): On 14th April 1984, a two car Class 108 diesel multiple unit calls at Northwich, which is situated between Chester and Manchester (Oxford Road), on the old CLC line. The colour light signal route indicator is for the freight only single line to Sandbach.
John Hillmer

Plate 42: A Class 47 loco-motive, No. 47224, passes through Lostock Gralam, on 10th December 1983, with 6H63, the 10.42 Appley Bridge to Northenden train, con-veying empty GMC refuse containers. These trains are routed via Northwich in order to avoid reversal at Warrington.

Paul Shannon

Plate 43: Another regular Saturday freight on the North-wich to Altrincham line is 6E47 the 11.08 Runcorn (Folly Lane) to Seal Sands working, which conveys ICI chemical tanks. It is seen approaching Plumley, on 10th December 1983, in the care of Class 40 No. 40160.

Paul Shannon

Plate 44 (above): In winter sunshine, Class 40 No. 40079 runs through Hale Station with a train load of limestone, bound for the ICI works at Northwich, on Guy Fawkes' Day, 1983.

John Hillmer

Plate 45 (right): Also pictured at Hale Station, but from a lower angle, Class 20 locomotives Nos. 20141 and 20077 are seen, on 30th May 1984, just a few weeks after having mainly displaced Class 25s, 40s and 47s from the ICI hopper trains.

John Hillmer

The Stockport Area

Plate 46: The trees were still bare when Class 25 No. 25235 passed through Northenden Junction, on 12th April 1984, with an inspection saloon. The siding and run-round facility on the right is the loading point for containerised GMC refuse trains, which run to the disposal area at Appley Bridge.

John Hillmer

Plate 47: On 22nd February 1983, Class 40s Nos. 40145 and 40172 pass Skelton Junction with 6H45, the 08.11 Widnes (Carterhouse Junction) to Topley Pike limestone empties. The line curving round to the right leads to Deansgate Junction and is used by freight trains for the Northwich direction.

Paul Shannon

Plate 48: On 19th November 1983, Class 45 'Peak' No. 45112 *The Royal Army Ordnance Corps* stands on one of the centre roads at Stockport (Edgeley) Station, waiting the arrival of a return excursion from London, which it will then take forward to Oldham.

John Hillmer

Plate 49: A two car diesel multiple unit arrives 'under the wires' at Stockport, on 4th July 1983, from Stalybridge. This short trip of 7½ miles enables passengers to and from West Yorkshire to avoid having to cross Manchester between Piccadilly and Victoria stations.

John Hillmer

Plate 50: Newly-named Class 56 locomotive No. 56124 *Blue Circle Cement* joins the main line at Stockport Edgeley Junction, after traversing the freight only line from Warrington Arpley, on 4th November 1983, with 6E33, the 10.55 Fiddler's Ferry to Healey Mills m.g.r. empties. Since closure of the Woodhead route, all such trains have been routed through Edgeley, continuing their journey via Denton, Guide Bridge and Stalybridge.

Paul Shannon

Plate 51: When the electrification was extended to Hazel Grove, the station was modernised, but the platform-mounted signal box remained. In this picture, taken in the late afternoon of 16th July 1984, the 16.58 diesel multiple unit service from Manchester (Piccadilly) calls on its way to Buxton.

John Hillmer

Plate 52 (above): Since electrification there have been few regular diesel-hauled trains through Wilmslow, but in the summer of 1979, there was a 09.28 (SO) Manchester (Piccadilly) to Newquay service which went via Hereford, and on 9th June Class 47 No. 47068 did the honours.
John Hillmer

Plate 53 (right): Class 40 No. 40035 speeds through Chelford, between Crewe and Manchester, on the evening of 7th July 1981, with a train of loaded ballast wagons.
John Hillmer

Plate 54 (left): Until May 1984, the Manchester to Cleethorpes/Hull services were worked by mixed formations of Trans-Pennine Class 124 and Inter-City Class 123 diesel multiple units. In this picture, taken on 5th July 1983, the 17.00 Hull to Manchester (Piccadilly) train takes the Reddish line at Romiley, and the unit comprises cars E52096, E59766, E59826 and E52091.

Paul Shannon

Plate 55 (below left): These Trans-Pennine services are now locomotive-hauled, usually with an e.t.h.-fitted Class 31 locomotive and four Mk. II coaches. Here, on 14th May 1984, the first day of the new timetable, No. 31406 approaches Bredbury with the 15.13 Hull to Manchester (Piccadilly). Note the trackbed of the former line to Stockport (Tiviot Dale) on the right.

Paul Shannon

Plate 56 (above): The 10.45 Manchester (Piccadilly) to Hull train, seen here between New Mills Central and New Mills South Junction, on 28th October 1982, is formed of a Class 123/4 unit, comprising cars E51961, E59770, E59825 and E52090.

Paul Shannon

Plate 57 (left): On 3rd March 1984 cars M54264 and M53970 form the 08.48 service to Manchester (Piccadilly) at Rose Hill, Marple, once a through station on the old LNER route from Manchester (then London Road) to Macclesfield (Central). Rose Hill became a terminus when the remainder of the line was closed in 1970.

John Hillmer

Plate 58: Saturday morning, 3rd March 1984, finds no passengers waiting to join the 09.37 diesel multiple unit from New Mills (Central) to Manchester (Piccadilly), as it stops briefly at Marple, although on weekdays these services are well partronised.

John Hillmer

Plate 59 (above): Class 25 No. 25134 heads the 6F42 Tunstead to Northwich limestone train towards New Mills on 28th October 1982. It has just left the main line at New Mills South Junction, and is now following the freight only route via Disley Tunnel.

Paul Shannon

Plate 60 (right): In the last years of Class 40 locomotives, the 08.14 summer 'Saturdays Only' train, from Manchester (Piccadilly) to Great Yarmouth, was often hauled by one of the remaining members of the class, thus becoming popular with 'haulage' enthusiasts. In this view, No. 40172 approaches Chinley on 30th July 1983.

John Hillmer

Lines to Buxton

Plate 61 (above): Another view of an ICI hopper train. On this occasion, on 4th June 1983, Class 25 No. 25133 hauls a set of empties past New Mills South Junction box. The line on the left is the old Midland route from Manchester (Central) but is now freight only from Skelton Junction, via Cheadle Heath. On the right is the main line to Manchester (Piccadilly), curving away to New Mills.
John Hillmer

Plate 63 (right): Class 45 'Peak' No. 45029 has just emerged from Dove Holes Tunnel with 6H30, the 13.23 Thorpes Bridge Junction to Tunstead limestone empties on 4th July 1983.
Paul Shannon

Plate 62 (left): On the last day of March 1983, a Class 104 three car diesel multiple unit, formed of cars M53556, M59228 and M53504, halts at Dove Holes, in the green rolling hills of Derbyshire, with the 08.53 Buxton to Manchester (Piccadilly) train. This is a passenger only route to Buxton contrasting with the freight only line to the famous spa town, from Chinley.
John Hillmer

Plate 64 (above): On 4th July 1983, Class 37 No. 37215 prepares to perform banking duties at the rear of 6J46, the 14.27 Peak Forest to Hope Street working. The train is headed by Class 37 locomotives Nos. 37080 and 37264, the regular motive power since the demise of Class 40s on this service.

Paul Shannon

Plate 65 (right): A Class 25 locomotive, No. 25326, arrives at Tunstead with the 9T34 trip working from Hindlow, on 4th July 1983. This must have been one of the last unfitted freight trains in the area, consisting of six vacuumpiped 'Covhops' (CHP), with two modern privately-owned hoppers (PAB) at the rear. After shunting at Peak Forest South, this train would have returned to Ashburys Yard.

Paul Shannon

Plate 66: Another view of the Hindlow trip freight (T34), this time seen at Hindlow itself, and after the introduction of high capacity air-braked wagons. Class 47 No. 47068 departs on the afternoon of 10th April 1984 with its one wagon destined for Barnby Dun Glassworks in South Yorkshire.

Paul Shannon

Plate 67: Saturday morning, 31st March 1984, sees Buxton Station with a full complement of Birmingham RC&W Class 104 units. The 08.25 to Manchester is seen leaving from platform 1. The diesel depot is adjacent to the station and there is activity seven days a week, with a variety of locomotives employed on freight duties.

John Hillmer

Manchester (Piccadilly)

Plate 68 (above): Since the inception of the May 1984 timetable, Class 31 locomotives are daily visitors to Manchester (Piccadilly), being used on four coach Mk. II sets to Cleethorpes and Hull. In this view, No. 31441 departs with 1E38, the 11.31 to Hull, on 30th May 1984.

John Hillmer

Plate 69 (right): With the May 1984 timetable, Piccadilly had its first regular HST Inter-City 125 services. On 9th August 1984, No. 43131 is the leading power car of the 10.39 to Plymouth.

John Hillmer

Plate 70: An interior view of Piccadilly Station, on 21st June 1984. A well-filled three car unit has just arrived from Buxton and will form the 15.18 return working. To the right stands a six car mixed formation, headed by car M51934 of a Derby-built Class 108 set.

John Hillmer

Plate 71: On 16th June 1984, a three car diesel multiple unit enters Manchester (Piccadilly) under the complexity of gantries and wires. Units work the routes to Buxton, to Rose Hill, Marple and to New Mills (Central), but no longer to Sheffield.

John Hillmer

Plate 72 (left): The only remaining link with St. Pancras is the 18.06 evening parcels train, and on this occasion Class 40 No. 40004 provides the motive power. It is photographed on 29th December 1983, with the use of a tripod and a time exposure.

John Hillmer

Plate 73 (below left): The two tracks between Piccadilly and Oxford Road stations are extremely busy with constant electric unit and diesel unit services, as well as Freightliner workings to and from Trafford Park Container Base. Oxford Road Station buildings have an unusually modernistic appearance. On 17th April 1984, a two car diesel multiple unit leaves for Manchester (Piccadilly) on the last leg of its journey from Liverpool (Lime Street), via Warrington (Central).

John Hillmer

Plate 74 (right): Class 40 No. 40135 approaches Guide Bridge Station, on 16th April 1984, with the daily cement working from Earles Sidings to Ashburys. Since closure of the Woodhead line, there is little necessity for changing locomotives, and the stabling point here is much less active.

John Hillmer

Plate 75 (below): Class 40 No. 40125 takes the goods lines at Guide Bridge on 17th September 1980, with a short eastbound train of empty BBA steel carriers.

Paul Shannon

Guide Bridge

Plate 76: Passing the site of Manchester (Exchange) Station, Class 47 No. 47473 approaches Manchester (Victoria) with the 08.05 Liverpool (Lime Street) to Newcastle train, on 3rd March 1984.

Paul Shannon

Plate 77: It was only towards the end of their working lives that Class 55 'Deltics' were to be seen in the north-west, and even then, irregularly, when they were based at York. In this scene, No. 55015 *Tulyar* is pictured leaving Manchester (Victoria) with the 13.05 Liverpool to Newcastle train on 10th June 1981.

John Hillmer

Plate 78 (above): Manchester (Victoria) Station's dark and dingy side platforms are used mainly by Oldham and Rochdale line services. Here, on 23rd September 1981, a Cravens two car unit departs with a Rochdale working, whist another Cravens unit and a Derby unit await their next turn of duty.

Paul Shannon

Plate 79 (right): Manchester (Victoria) sees considerable through freight traffic and Class 25 No. 25296 is seen coming in from the east with two vans, bound for Bolton, on 22nd June 1983.

John Hillmer

Plate 80: At the west end of Manchester (Victoria) Station, on 1st May 1981, Class 25 No. 25132 stands with the Springs Branch (Wigan) rerailing unit.

John Hillmer

Plate 81: Class 47 No. 47298 passes West Junction box as it enters Manchester (Victoria) on 23rd July 1984, at the head of 1E08, the 08.47 Holyhead to Newcastle working, from the west to the east coast of Britain.

John Hillmer

Plate 82: On 10th June 1981, Class 40 No. 40178 runs down the bank from Miles Platting into the station area with a tanker train. In the reverse direction some freights continue to be banked, normally by a Class 25 locomotive but more recently by a Class 31.

John Hillmer

Plate 83: A Class 128 Gloucester RC&W Motor Parcels Van, No. M55993, shows a turn of speed through Manchester (Victoria) Station on 26th May 1983.

John Hillmer

Eastwards from Victoria

Plate 84 (above): Class 47 No. 47029 hauls 6E36, the 07.00 Holyhead to Immingham oil empties, up the bank from Victoria to Collyhurst Street on 26th April 1984.
Paul Shannon

Plate 85 (below): Seen through a rather depleted signal gantry at Collyhurst Street, Class 45 'Peak' No. 45142 climbs Miles Platting Bank with the 08.05 Liverpool (Lime Street) to Newcastle train on 26th April 1984.
Paul Shannon

Plate 86: Class 46 'Peak' No.46047 was an unusual visitor to Manchester on 26th April 1984 when it worked 8M08, the 10.52 Healey Mills to Ashburys freight. It is seen passing Philips Park No. 1 box, shortly after some rationalisation of the signalling, and with further trackwork reductions imminent.
Paul Shannon

Plate 87: Class 47 No. 47430 slows for the severe curve into Miles Platting Station on 26th April 1984, whilst heading the 07.05 Liverpool (Lime Street) to Scarborough service. The goods lines on the left are now disused and will shortly be lifted, possibly to make way for a realigned main line.
Paul Shannon

Plate 90 (right): Seen passing Diggle Junction box, on 29th October 1982, Class 56 No. 56074 *Kellingley Colliery* heads 6M51, the 11.39 Healey Mills to Fiddler's Ferry m.g.r. train.

Paul Shannon

Plate 91 (below right): On the first day of June 1981, a Class 47 locomotive, No. 47447, passes over the scenically-situated Saddleworth Viaduct, between Huddersfield and Stalybridge, with a York to Liverpool (Lime Street) train.

John Hillmer

Plate 88: Class 25 No. 25214 is pictured towing Great Northern suburban unit No. 313026 past Thorpes Bridge Junction on 25th March 1981. The unit is returning to the Eastern Region after overhaul at Horwich Works, and is now on its way to Healey Mills, via Hebden Bridge.

Paul Shannon

Plate 89: Class 37 No. 37082 takes an eastbound tank train over Droylsden Viaduct on 26th April 1984.

Paul Shannon

Over The Pennines — via Diggle . . .

. . . and via Todmorden

Plate 94 (right): Birmingham RC&W power cars M53444 and M53500 form the 09.28 Manchester (Victoria)—Rochdale—Oldham—Manchester (Victoria) service on 29th October 1983. It is seen between Shaw and Royton Junction. Most services on this route are worked by two power cars with no intermediate trailer car, to provide sufficient power for the severe gradients.

Paul Shannon

Plate 95 (below right): Another view of the Oldham loop, but this time a Swindon cross country unit is, rather unusually, working the 13.28 Manchester (Victoria)—Rochdale—Oldham—Manchester (Victoria) service. The scene was captured on 29th October 1983, just south of Shaw Station.

Paul Shannon

Plate 92: A four car Eastern Region Derby-built unit passes Vitriol Works box, near Middleton, on a Leeds—Bradford—Manchester working on the morning of 12th September 1981.

Paul Shannon

Plate 93: A Calder Valley unit, comprising cars E51826, E59810 and E51835, leaves Todmorden with the 15.29 Leeds to Manchester (Victoria) working on 25th April 1984.

Paul Shannon

Salford

Plate 96: Seen from the fourteenth floor of a tower block, Class 40 No. 40168 passes through Salford Station, on 26th April 1984, with 6F32, the 19.02 Ashburys to Walton Old Junction 'Speedlink' train.

Paul Shannon

Plate 97: Class 47 No. 47142 heads 4D59, the 15.54 Trafford Park to Holyhead Freightliner past Ordsall Lane Junction on 26th April 1984. The lines to the right, in the background, lead to Manchester (Oxford Road), via Castlefield Junction.

Paul Shannon

Plate 98: Class 40 No. 40009 is seen passing Agecroft Junction with 4J17, the 06.30 Barrow to Red Bank parcels working, on 26th April 1984, having deposited most of its load at Bolton.

Paul Shannon

Plate 99: Class 47 No. 47459 heads the southbound 'European', the 11.06 Edinburgh/11.20 Glasgow (Central) to Harwich (Parkeston Quay) train, past Windsor Bridge Junction on 26th April 1984.

Paul Shannon

Plate 101 (above right): Class 47 locomotive No. 47532 passes the disused Brindle Heath Sidings signal box, whilst hauling the 17.15 Manchester (Victoria) to Blackpool (North) service on 26th April 1984.

Paul Shannon

Plate 102 (right): The short stretch of line between Brindle Heath Junction and Agecroft Junction is due for closure, and a new station is to be built on the fast lines at Pendleton. At Brindle Heath Junction, on 12th September 1981, a Derby two car set heads north with a Manchester to Blackburn working. *Paul Shannon*

Plate 100 (left): On 12th September 1981, a six car mixed diesel multiple unit formation approaches Brindle Heath Sidings with an afternoon Blackpool to Manchester working, and follows the fast lines which avoid Pendleton Station. *Paul Shannon*

Plate 103 (left): The disused Kearsley Power-Station and the M62 motorway form a backdrop to this view of Class 40 No. 40079 with 4J17, the Barrow to Red Bank parcels working, on 27th October 1982. The receding diesel multiple unit is on a Manchester to Blackpool service, and the vantage point is near Pepper Hill box, Clifton.
Paul Shannon

Plate 104 (below left): Class 47 No. 47515 is dwarfed by Kearsley's cooling towers, as it heads north with the 17.15 Manchester (Victoria) to Blackpool (North) train on 26th June 1984.
Paul Shannon

Plate 105 (right): During 1984, Longsight's allocation of Class 25s was gradually replaced by a small fleet of Class 31 locomotives. This view shows No. 31149 shunting Bolton Goods Yard on 23rd May 1984, before leaving with the 6T85 trip freight to Ashburys.

Paul Shannon

Plate 106 (below): Class 40 No. 40009 approaches Bolton (East) with 4J14, the 13.58 Preston to Red Bank parcels train, on 28th April 1984. The train comprises no less than 22 vehicles, which is quite normal for this service.
Paul Shannon

Plate 107 (left): A Derby-built diesel multiple unit forms the 14.55 Manchester (Victoria) to Blackburn service, as it leaves Bolton Station on 28th April 1984.

Paul Shannon

Plate 108 (below): A total of thirteen GMC refuse trains each week are scheduled to serve Appley Bridge disposal point; seven from Dean Lane and six from Northenden. The Dean Lane trains are always routed via Bolton, and in this picture Class 40 No. 40060 is seen passing Lostock Junction with 6J75, the 09.57 Appley Bridge to Dean Lane, on 25th April 1984.

Paul Shannon

Plate 109: After a light fall of snow, on 24th January 1984, Class 47 No. 47532 approaches Lostock Junction with the northbound 'European', the 07.17 Harwich (Parkeston Quay) to Edinburgh/Glasgow (Central) train.

Paul Shannon

Plate 110: A busy few minutes at Blackrod, between Bolton and Chorley, on 10th June 1983, as Class 47 No. 47534 with 2J13, the 12.45 Blackpool (North) to Manchester (Victoria) train, stops simultaneously with the 13.17 diesel multiple unit service on a reverse working.

John Hillmer

Plate 111: A Derby Class 108 unit, comprising cars M51563 and M53930, forms the 15.35 Blackburn to Manchester (Victoria) train as it prepares to stop at Bromley Cross, near Bolton, on 24th April 1984.

John Hillmer

Plate 112: On 25th April 1984, the 11.33 Blackburn to Manchester (Victoria) working is composed of Birmingham RC&W power cars M53527 and M53475, as it crosses Astley Bridge Viaduct on the approaches to Bolton.

Paul Shannon

Plate 113: Newly built at Crewe, Class 56 locomotive No. 56132 approaches Warrington (Bank Quay) with a light load of one 'Cargowaggon', on 18th July 1984.

John Hillmer

Plate 114: The West Coast Main Line through Warrington sees considerable freight traffic; much of it diesel-hauled. In this scene, Class 40 No. 40035 *Apapa* waits for a signal on the 'up' side of Bank Quay Station with a train of tank wagons bound for Stanlow.

John Hillmer

Plate 115 (above left): Class 08 shunter No. 08838 shunts PCA cement wagons into the Blue Circle terminal at Tanhouse Lane, Widnes, on 7th July 1983. These wagons would have arrived on 7F39, the 07.40 Earles Sidings to Widnes train, and the empties would return to the Hope Valley on 6H33, the 12.02 departure from Widnes.

Paul Shannon

Plate 116 (below left):Running beneath Warrington (Bank Quay) Station, Class 31 locomotives, Nos. 31259 and 31249 bring through the 6H33 empties on 24th July 1984. Within a few hundred yards, it will pass Arpley stabling point and the link to the marshalling yard at Warrington, which in turn is connected to the West Coast Main Line, enabling transfer of freight trains to take place, when required.

John Hillmer

Plate 117 (above): On 22nd February 1983, Class 56 No. 56020 heads 6M51, the 11.39 Healey Mills to Fiddler's Ferry m.g.r. train, and is pictured passing over the threatened Manchester Ship Canal bridge at Latchford near Warrington.

Paul Shannon

Plate 118 (below): Class 47 No. 47356 passes Sinderland Crossing, between Skelton Junction and Lymm, with the late-running 6M62, 20.53 Harwich (Parkeston Quay) to Widnes 'Speedlink' service, on 10th December 1983. Currently this stretch of line is scheduled to be used by 17 freight trains in each direction each day.

Paul Shannon

Eastwards from Liverpool

Plate 119: Class 45 'Peak' No. 45139 approaches Newton-le-Willows on 24th July 1984, with 1E08, the 08.47 Holyhead to Newcastle service.

John Hillmer

Plate 120: On 27th April 1984, Class 45 'Peak' No. 45057 heads the 09.05 Liverpool (Lime Street) to Scarborough train through Huyton.

Paul Shannon

Plate 121:   On the bright Easter Monday of 1984, an eight car unit, led by Class 108, car M53934, calls at St. Helens Junction with an excursion from Liverpool (Lime Street) to Blackpool.

John Hillmer

Plate 122:   On 23rd April 1984, Class 45 'Peak' No. 45120 stops at St. Helens Junction with 1E06, the 09.05 Liverpool (Lime Street) to Scarborough train. On the right are Bold Colliery sidings, used for the stabling of the locomotives used during the Rainhill Celebrations in 1980.

John Hillmer

Plate 123: The 07.47 Kirkby to Wigan (Wallgate) train arrives at Rainford on 27th April 1984, formed by the unique combination of cars M53355 and M53812 — the last surviving Gloucester RC&W car coupled to the last Manchester-based Cravens car.

Paul Shannon

Plate 124 (left): On a bright morning in April 1984, Class 40 locomotive No. 40015 rushes through Rainhill Station with 1E79, the 10.05 Liverpool to Scarborough service.

John Hillmer

Plate 125 (right): A diversion in the snow. Class 47 No. 47483 departs from St. Helens (Shaw Street) with the 12.19 York to Liverpool (Lime Street) train on Sunday, 22nd January 1984; it has been routed this way due to engineering work on the main line. In the distance, the 15.00 Liverpool (Lime Street) to Newcastle working can be seen leaving for Manchester, which it will reach by way of Bamfurlong, Golborne and Parkside junctions.

Paul Shannon

Plate 126 (left): Class 47 No. 47411 enters the long tunnel and cutting towards Edge Hill, as it leaves Liverpool (Lime Street), bound for Newcastle, on 29th July 1982.

John Hillmer

Plate 128 (right): Class 40 No. 40012 leaves Aintree with 6F63 the 11.07 Aintree to Edge Hill working, on 7th July 1983, conveying four VDAs from the Metal Box Factory. There is no physical connection at Aintree between the freight line and the electrified passenger line (which can be seen on the right of the picture), and all freight traffic is routed via Marsh Lane Junction and Bootle.

Paul Shannon

Plate 127 (below): Under the impressive roof of Lime Street Station, on 17th April 1984, five sets of diesel multiple units can be seen, with Class 45 'Peak' No. 45139 stabled at the buffer stops awaiting its next turn of duty.

John Hillmer

Ormskirk Preston & north ↘

Plate 129 (below): The BICC factory at Prescot is still rail-connected, and receives traffic from abroad in high capacity ferry wagons. This picture, taken on 27th April 1984, shows Class 25 No. 25315 waiting to leave with T75, the trip freight to Warrington. The chemical tank wagon was picked up earlier in the day from the Leathers factory in St. Helens.

Paul Shannon

Plate 130:   Passing under one of the few remaining signal gantries on Merseyside, Class 47 No. 47091 approaches Bootle Junction with 9L44, an engineer's special working from Fazakerley to Northwich.

Paul Shannon

Plate 131 (above right):   Metropolitan-Cammell Class 101 unit, comprising cars E51499 and E51433, ticks over in Southport Station, on 22nd August 1984, and forms the 11.25 to York.

John Hillmer

Plate 132 (below right):   With the exception of the electrified line to Liverpool (Central), Southport has only diesel multiple unit services to Manchester (Victoria), with a few of these trains, each day, going on to Leeds or York. The 13.40 service to Leeds leaves a cloud of exhaust as it departs on a sunny 3rd April 1984.

Paul Shannon

Plate 133: A Birmingham RC&W unit, comprising cars M53454 and M53528, forms the 11.16 Southport to Manchester (Victoria) train at Bescar Lane on 5th June 1983.

Paul Shannon

Plate 134: Douglas Bank signal box is just west of Wigan, on the Southport line, and survives to serve the GKN factory sidings there. In this view, photographed on 19th May 1984, the 11.25 Southport to York train is worked by a four car unit, comprising cars M53983, M54266, E51834 and E52068.

Paul Shannon

Plate 135: Class 47 No. 47364 passes through Gathurst, on 19th May 1984, with 6H63, the 10.42 (SO) Appley Bridge to Northenden working, conveying empty GMC refuse containers. On the right of the picture is the former station goods yard, now used as private sidings for the local ICI works, and served by a regular trip freight from Warrington.

Paul Shannon

Plate 136 (above): On 12th Ma
1984, the 11.40 Southport t
Manchester (Victoria) train leave
Wigan (Wallgate) and is forme
of diesel multiple unit car
M53466 and M54180.

Paul Shanno

Plate 137 (left): On 25th Jul
1984, a two car diesel multipl
unit, comprising cars M5393
and M51570, stands in the bay a
Wigan (North Western) Statio
and forms the 11.22 service t
Liverpool (Lime Street). Behin
the unit can be seen the unusua
octagonal-shaped waiting-room.

John Hillme

Plate 138: A Swindon cross-country unit, formed of cars M51783, M59683 and M51792, is seen passing over the Leeds and Liverpool Canal, near Ince-in-Makerfield, on 31st October 1983, again working the 11.40 Southport to Manchester (Victoria) service.

Paul Shannon

Plate 139 (below): An eight car Metropolitan-Cammell diesel multiple unit passes the rare 'gallows' type signal at Atherton, whilst working the 09.29 Leeds to Southport service on 28th April 1984. The signal box at this location is now, more or less, permanently switched out, and preparations can be seen in the centre of the picture for relaying this stretch of line as a single track.

Paul Shannon

Plate 140 (above left): The line between Farington Curve Junction and Midge Hall has recently been singled — notice the position of the new colour light signal! However, the signal box survives as a fringe box to the Preston power box area, as well as to control the level crossing. A Derby two car unit, comprising cars M54501 and M53944, is seen working the 11.20 Preston to Ormskirk service on 9th July 1983, as the signalman hands over the token for the section to Rufford.

Paul Shannon

Plate 141 (below left): The 12.57 Preston to Ormskirk train arrives at Rufford on 12th March 1983, operated by the same two car unit as seen above, but in reverse formation.

Paul Shannon

Plate 142 (right): Class 47 No. 47422 of Gateshead, stops in Chorley Station with the 12.45 Blackpool (North) to Manchester (Victoria) working, on 4th April 1984. The wheel controlling the crossing gates can just be seen in the box.

John Hillmer

Plate 143 (below): One locomotive-hauled set of Mk. I coaches is used to supplement the diesel multiple unit service between Manchester and Blackpool. On 3rd April 1984, Class 47 No. 47497 pulls out from Chorley Station with the 12.45 Blackpool (North) to Manchester (Victoria) train.

Paul Shannon

Preston

Plate 144 (left): A two car unit enters Preston, at the north end, and will form the 12.57 to Ormskirk, on 21st November 1983. Preston also acts as the starting point for the diesel multiple unit services to Colne, and a few of the services to Blackpool (South) and to Barrow-in-Furness.

John Hillmer

Plate 146 (above right): Class 47 No. 47193 leaves the bright sunshine for the shadows of Preston Station, as it coasts through with a 'down' train of empty BBA steel carriers, on 21st November 1983.

John Hillmer

Plate 147 (below right): Preston Station pilot, Class 08 shunter No. 08297, shunts a TPO coach at Preston on 21st November 1983. In the background can be seen the locomotive stabling point which often contains members of Classes 25, 40 and 47.

John Hillmer

Plate 145 (right): Preston is an important location for the changing from electric traction to diesel, and vice versa. This is required on a variety of services going forward to, or coming from, the non-electrified lines to Manchester, Liverpool, Blackpool (North) and Barrow. No change was necessary in this scene, as Class 47 No. 47437 is working through with 1P11, the 11.30 Liverpool (Lime street) to Barrow train, on 22nd September 1983.

John Hillmer

East Lancashire Lines

Plate 148 (above): The line between Preston and Colne passes through delightful countryside. On 10th July 1981, a two car diesel multiple unit is seen leaving Pleasington with a Preston to Colne service, which runs via Blackburn.

John Hillme

Plate 149 (left): Also at Pleasington, an unidentified Class 25 locomotive, with a train of empty wagons, hurries through the station, towards Blackburn, on a sunny August day in 1983.

John Hillme

Plate 150 (right): A two car diesel unit, comprising cars M50493 and M50520, pauses at the remote station of Entwistle whilst working the 13.33 Blackburn to Manchester (Victoria service on 30th June 1982.

Paul Shannon

Plate 151: A busy scene at Blackburn on 22nd August 1983. The two car unit in the bay is bound for Manchester (Victoria), whilst on the through line the Class 104 Birmingham RC&W unit, leaves for Preston. Stabled on the right is a Class 37 locomotive, No. 37018, which, together with a sister locomotive alongside, will take a train of loaded cement wagons north, to Horrocksford Cement Works. In the background a Class 25 locomotive shunts in the yard.

John Hillmer

Plate 152: P. & G. Fogarty's distribution depot at Blackburn provides enough rail traffic to warrant a daily 'Speedlink' train to Warrington. On 31st May 1984, Class 47 No. 47075 failed before working this service, and help had to be summoned in the shape of Class 25 No. 25072.

Paul Shannon

Plate 153: The Blackburn to Hellifield line is still double track, but traffic along it is considerably reduced since the decline of the Settle & Carlisle line. The Ribble Cement works at Horrocksford, near Clitheroe, sends two or three trains a week to Gunnie (routed via Preston and the West Coast Main Line), and, usually, one train to Newcastle (routed via Skipton and the East Coast Main Line). Here, Class 37s Nos. 37067 and 37059 are seen crossing Whalley Arches with the 6S83 Clitheroe to Gunnie working on 1st July 1983.

Michael Rhodes

Plate 154: Class 40 No. 40136 heads east through Blackburn Station, on 23rd September 1981, with a Class 8 freight bound for Carlisle.

Paul Shannon

Plate 155: The line from Gannow Junction to Colne was left out of the Preston resignalling scheme in the early 1970s, and thus retains manual signalling, with boxes at Burnley (Central), Brierfield and Chaffers Siding. However, plans are afoot to reduce the whole line to a single track from Gannow Junction. On 30th May 1983, the 11.48 Colne to Preston train leaves Burnley (Central), and is composed of diesel multiple unit cars M53443, M53493, M53525 and M53473.

Paul Shannon

Plate 156: A Birmingham RC&W unit, comprising cars M50500 and M50444, leaves Brierfield with the 13.46 Colne to Preston service on 30th May 1983.

Paul Shannon

Plate 157: The Colne branch is already single track beyond the level crossing at Chaffers Siding, near Nelson. In this view, taken at Chaffers Siding on 30th May 1983, the 12.41 Colne to Preston train is formed of a pair of Derby two car units, comprising cars M54246, M53982, M53963 and M54240.

Paul Shannon

Plate 158 (below): The Copy Pit line has had mixed fortunes in recent years. It was resignalled and upgraded as part of the Preston power box scheme in the early 1970s, when freight traffic between Healey Mills and Blackburn was quite heavy, although the passenger service was limited to a handful of summer Saturday holiday trains to Blackpool. Then in 1982, all freight traffic was diverted away from the line, and Blackburn started receiving its coal via Warrington, and the Preston Docks oil trains were sent via Manchester. Since May 1984 the line has seen a slightly improved passenger service, with a daily Bradford to Preston diesel multiple unit service sponsored by the National & Provincial Building Society. This scene, photographed on a misty Saturday, 9th June 1984, shows Class 37 No. 37032 climbing through Cornholme with the dated 07.49 Sheffield to Blackpool (North) working.

Paul Shannon

Preston to Blackpool

Plate 159: Since this view was photographed, the Blackpool (South) branch has been reduced to a single track. A two car unit, comprising cars M53453 and M53520, is seen leaving St. Anne's Station with the 15.55 Blackpool (South) to Kirkham service on 9th July 1983.

Paul Shannon

Plate 160 (left): Class 40s were still regular visitors to Blackpool (North) on summer Saturday holiday trains during 1983. On 9th July 1983, Class 40 No. 40177 worked the 14.28 Blackpool (North) to Edinburgh train, and is seen approaching Weeton.

Paul Shannon

Plate 161: On 27th April 1984, and dominated by the famous Blackpool Tower, Swindon Class 120 unit, headed by car M51589, takes the 09.07 service to Manchester (Victoria), and is seen at Blackpool (North).

John Hillmer

Plate 162: Class 37 No. 37121 arrives at Blackpool (North) with the 09.21 from Sheffield on 4th September 1982. This train has followed an unusual route from Sheffield, via Wakefield, Elland, Hebden Bridge and Blackburn, and is the only scheduled locomotive hauled train over the Copy Pit line.

Paul Shannon

Plate 163: Two three car Birmingham RC&W units are seen working the 13.45 Manchester (Victoria) to Blackpool (North) train on 4th September 1982. The location is Poulton-le-Fylde, where the little-used freight line to Fleetwood diverges.

Paul Shannon

Plate 164: This is the return working of the train pictured in *Plate 162*, the 13.59 Blackpool (North) to Sheffield service. It is seen passing the delapidated signal box at Weeton, on 9th July 1983.

Paul Shannon

Lancaster

Plate 165 (above): Class 40 No. 40168 was in charge of 1P35, the 15.13 Crewe to Barrow service, on 7th August 1984, and is seen leaving Lancaster Station. The freight train on the left, which was held in the 'down' through road, was also Class 40-hauled!
John Hillmer

Plate 166 (left): The 18.57 diesel multiple unit service to More-cambe, on the left, and the 17.25 from Barrow, on the right, stand in the 'down' side bay platforms at Lancaster Station, on 25th February 1984.

John Hillmer

Heysham to Skipton

Plate 167 (left): Class 31 locomotives Nos. 31275 and 31200 pass through Wennington with 7E91, the 12.02 Heysham Moss to Haverton Hill ammonia train, on Saturday, 9th June 1984. This train runs six days a week, and is the only regular freight on the Lancaster to Settle line, apart from occasional oil trains from Stanlow to Skipton.

Paul Shannon

Plate 169 (right): A four car Metropolitan-Cammell unit approaches Wennington Station with the 12.35 Leeds to Morecambe service, on 11th July 1983.

Paul Shannon

Plate 170 (below right): In May 1984, a new through service between Hull and Lancaster was introduced. There are three trains in each direction every weekday, using Class 31/4 locomotives and 5 coach rakes of Mk. 1 stock. This picture shows No. 31440, near Clapham, with the 13.36 Lancaster to Hull train, on 9th June 1984.

Paul Shannon

Plate 168 (below): Class 40 No. 40150 arrives at Heysham Moss ICI sidings, on 11th July 1983, with 7M37, the 03.40 from Haverton Hill, this being the return working of the train pictured above. Notice the ex-ferry van in use as a barrier vehicle behind the locomotive.

Paul Shannon

Plate 171: On a bright spring day at Morecambe, in April 1984, a Class 108 Derby-built two car unit, headed by car E53614, has just arrived from Lancaster, to where it will shortly return.

John Hillmer

Plate 172: Showing the long capacity platforms at Morecambe Station, with the large signal box, a two car diesel multiple unit arrives from Lancaster, whilst the 13.42 service to Leeds stands on the left on 25th April 1984.

John Hillmer

Carnforth to Barrow

Plate 173: On the first day of May 1984, Silverdale Station (between Lancaster and Barrow) sees Class 25 locomotive No. 25324 with a single tank wagon, heading south. The station building now houses a suitably-named restaurant called 'Coppernobs'!

John Hillmer

Plate 174: On 14th July 1983, Class 40 No. 40057 approaches Silverdale a.h.b. crossing with 6F58, the 14.51 Corkickle to Northwich sodium carbonate working.

Paul Shannon

Plate 175 (above): Class 25 No. 25089 heads east through Ulverston Station with an empty spoil train, on the morning of 12th July 1983.

Paul Shannon

Plate 176 (left): A clear road for the 12.14 diesel multiple unit service from Carlisle to Lancaster, as it approaches Black Dyke Crossing, just south of Arnside, on 1st May 1984.

John Hillmer

Plate 177: On 14th July 1983, Class 25 No. 25221 shunts MCV and HTV coal wagons at Hackett Coal Depot, on the Barrow-in-Furness docks branch. After shunting at the Hackett siding, the locomotive will propel the remaining wagons down the branch to Cart Coal Depot, which is just visible on the left of the picture. Both Hackett and Cart depots were closed during 1984 since they are unable to accommodate modern air-braked hopper wagons.

Paul Shannon

Plate 178: On 14th July 1983, Class 47 No. 47281 takes the straight ahead route at Salthouse Junction, Barrow-in-Furness, to gain access to the docks branch. The train is 9P36, the 06.42 Walton Old Junction to Carlisle working, which will later reverse back out of the sidings and continue north, via Whitehaven and Workington.

Paul Shannon

The Cumbrian Coast Line

Plate 181 (right): Nuclear waste trains run to Sellafield from a number of different locations, including Valley (Anglesey), Bridgwater and Fairlie. In this view, photographed on 12th July 1983, Class 25 No. 25089 passes through Bootle with 7V41, the 17.22 Sellafield to Bridgwater return empties working.

Paul Shannon

Plate 182 (below right): Class 40 No. 40152 crosses the estuary at Eskmeals with 6F58, the 14.51 Corkickle to Northwich chemical tanks, on 12th July 1983.

Paul Shannon

Plate 179 (left): Class 47 No. 47441 leaves Barrow-in-Furness Station with the 13.10 to Liverpool (Lime Street) on 14th July 1983.

Paul Shannon

Plate 180 (below): The 13.47 diesel unit from Whitehaven arrives at Barrow, on 7th August 1984, behind the rear coach of the 15.24 service to Crewe.

John Hillmer

Plate 183 (left): Because of restricted clearances, no locomotive-hauled passenger trains can run along the Cumbrian Coast line and the diesel multiple units operating this service have metal bars protecting all opening windows. The bars on cars M54243 and M53959 are clearly visible, as this unit pauses at Millom with the 12.08 Lancaster to Whitehaven service, on 12th July 1983.

Paul Shannon

Plate 184 (right): Two collieries remain connected to the Cumbrian Coast line — Haig Colliery, at Whitehaven, and Lakeland Colliery, near Maryport. In this scene, photographed on 13th July 1983, Class 40 No. 40082 departs north from Workington with a train of empty HAA wagons for Maryport.

Paul Shannon

Plate 185 (below): The 13.10 service from Carlisle near the end of its journey at Whitehaven, on 13th July 1983, is formed of a Derby two car unit, comprising cars M53980 and M54256.

Paul Shannon

Plate 186: Passing beneath the loader at Lakeland Colliery is Class 40 No. 40129 with 6P49, the 06.55 m.g.r. empties from Workington, on 13th July 1983. After loading, this train will return south as 7F22, the 08.33 Maryport to Fiddler's Ferry working.

Paul Shannon

Plate 187: Class 37 locomotives Nos. 37079 and 37042 head 4E36, the 09.30 Workington to Lackenby steel empties through Maryport Station, on 13th July 1983. Notice the unusual track layout, with only the right-hand line having platform access.

Paul Shannon

Plate 188 (above right): Skipton Station retains a delightful atmosphere, with ornate platform canopies and wooden-posted semaphore signals. A two car diesel multiple unit, comprising cars E50601 and E56201, is seen departing west with the 14.31 Leeds to Morecambe service, on 26th March 1983.

Paul Shannon

Plate 189 (below right): This view shows the other end of Skipton Station, on 26th March 1983, with Class 47 No. 47005 heading the 10.00 Carlisle to Leeds train. On the left is the tail end of a Carlisle-bound freight train, which has been stabled at Skipton over the weekend.

Paul Shannon

Skipton

Plate 190: Just after the long rail strike of summer 1982, and ten months before the end of regular freight workings over the Settle & Carlisle route, Class 40 No. 40196 passes Settle Junction with the 6M64 Healey Mills to Carlisle working on the evening of 20th July 1982.

Paul Shannon

Plate 191: Pen-y-Ghent provides the backdrop for Class 40 No. 40169 as it approaches Selside on 20th July 1982, with 6S35, the 15.30 Burn Naze to Stevenson ICI chemical train. This train ran once a week, and followed a route from the Fleetwood branch, through Blackburn and Hellifield, to Carlisle.

Paul Shannon

Plate 192: Seen through a 200mm. lens, from a vantage point near Arten Gill Viaduct, Class 47 No. 47248 heads south from Dent Station with the 06.55 Glasgow (Central) to Nottingham train on 20th August 1981.

Paul Shannon

Plate 193: Class 25 No. 25256 passes over Arten Gill Viaduct on 20th August 1981 with the daily Severn Tunnel Junction to Carlisle 'Speedlink' train. This train was diverted to run via Shap in May 1982, leaving only vacuum-braked freights on the Settle & Carlisle route.

Paul Shannon

Plate 194: During the summer of 1983, Kingmoor's green-liveried Class 40 locomotive, No. 40122, was a common sight on the Carlisle to Leeds trains. It is seen returning north with the 16.00 Leeds to Carlisle service on 18th August of that year.

Paul Shannon

Plate 195: Class 25 No. 25271 approaches Appleby Station, on 18th August 1981, with 8E15, the 14.43 Carlisle to Healey Mills working. The lines to the right are now used for access to the military depot at Warcop, and it is intended to keep the line from Carlisle to Appleby open to serve this depot.

Paul Shannon

The Windermere Branch

Plate 196: In the hills of Cumbria, a two car diesel multiple unit leaves Staveley, on 1st May 1984, with the 14.08 from Oxenholme to Winderemere. The terminus at Winderemere is undergoing a complete refurbishment.
John Hillmer

Carlisle

Plate 199 (right):   Class 27 No. 27014 has just brought in a 'McAlpine Charter' from Scotland, on 19th July 1984, whilst Class 40 No. 40150 waits to take the train on via the Settle & Carlisle route. Class 27s (and 26s) are regular visitors to Carlisle, often being used on the diesel-hauled trains to and from Glasgow (Central), via Dumfries.

John Hillmer

Plate 200 (below right):   Class 40 No. 40007 heads north, on 24th August 1981, along the Carlisle avoiding line, with a short nuclear flask train from Sellafield.

Paul Shannon

Plate 197 (left):   Class 47 No. 47533 leaves Carlisle (Citadel) Station with the 10.40 to Leeds, on 21st June 1984. At this time, with threat of closure hanging heavily over the Settle & Carlisle route, there are only two passenger trains scheduled in each direction daily, Sundays excepted.

John Hillmer

Plate 198 (below):   On 19th July 1984, the driver of Class 08 shunter, No. 08912, watches intently as he backs two GUVs into one of the two 'up' side bays, at the south end of Carlisle (Citadel) Station. These platforms are used by the Newcastle trains that are operated by diesel multiple units.

John Hillmer

Plate 201: On a beautifully clear afternoon, in April 1963, Class 40 No. D325 is seen at Greenholme with the 11.20 Birmingham (New Street) to Glasgow (Central) and Edinburgh train.

John S. Whiteley

Plates 202 & 203: As mentioned in the introduction, the West Coast Main Line was used for testing Britain's first main line diesels. On the right, LMS locomotives Nos. 10000 and 10001 are seen near Shap with the 'down' 'Royal Scot' express, whilst the left-hand picture shows SR locomotive No. 10203 on the corresponding 'up' working. Both photographs were taken during May 1957.

Robert Leslie

Plate 204: On 18th May 1971, Class 50 locomotives Nos. 410 and 419 head the 12.00 Glasgow
(Central) to London (Euston) train round the curve
at Oxenholme.

J. H. Cooper-Smith

Plate 205: The 'up' 'Royal Scot' is seen south of
Oxenholme in May 1972, with Class 50 No. 404
leading. Waiting in the loop is an unidentified
Class 25 locomotive, at the head of a local trip
freight from Kendal, on the Windermere branch.

J. H. Cooper-Smith

Plate 206 (left): Dillicar water troughs were still in position on 27th June 1964, when Class 40 No. D336 passed through with the 09.30 Manchester (Victoria) to Glasgow (Central) train.
John S. Whiteley

Plate 207 (right): A two car Derby lightweight diesel multiple unit climbs away from the West Coast Main Line at Penrith, on 13th April 1957, heading for Workington, via Keswick. Note the original green livery, complete with front end chevrons.
Robert Leslie

Plate 208 (left): A two tone-liveried Class 47, No. D1866, threads its way through the Lune Gorge with a Birmingham to Glasgow working, on 22nd July 1967.
J. H. Cooper-Smith